As a pastor, I realize that the most important thing we can do is help the next generation embrace the Good News of what Jesus accomplished for us on the cross. Likewise, I expect that as a parent, you want to be sure to introduce your children to the story of the crucifixion in a way that will touch them personally but will be appropriate for their stage of development. This is why I am glad to endorse Sofia and the Tree, a tale about a caring little girl who has a unique perspective of the cross. This wonderful book can help you as a parent share what Jesus did on the cross in a way that your children can understand and that will help them love the Savior.

Dr. Charles F. Stanley

The founder of In Touch Ministries and a New York Times best-selling author

Many, many years ago, in the city of Jerusalem, there lived a little girl named Sofia. Sofia's family was very poor, but that never stopped her from being happy. Life in those days was not easy. The people of Jerusalem were under the rule of the great Roman Empire, which was not kind to the people.

When Sofia's birthday came, she knew that her family was not able to give her much, but she was just happy to be turning six years old. To her surprise, her mom came home with a very special gift.

"Sofia," her mommy called loudly. "Come see what I have for you!" Sofia ran to her mother as fast as she could.

Sofia's mom gave her the gift—a little tree. Sofia was very excited! She started calling out names for the tree and wondered where she would plant such a great gift.

She ran outside and
began digging with her
hands. Soon she had a
hole big enough to plant
the tree.

Every day, Sofia watered her tree, played by the tree, and occasionally, she *even* talked to the tree. This tree was very special to Sofia.

She cared so much for the tree that, at times, she would fall asleep by the tree, dreaming that one day it would grow big and tall, all the way to heaven.

The days and years went by, and the tree grew tall and strong. Sofia never missed a day watering her tree. She enjoyed her tree. In the summer, the tree gave her shade and, in the fall, beautiful colors. In her mind, Sofia would still get lost daydreaming about her tree reaching up to heaven. As the tree grew, so did Sofia.

Jerusalem continued to be under the ruthless control of the Roman Empire, which continued to overtax the people, making them poorer every day.

Sofia's family suffered, so she made a very difficult decision to help her family. She decided to sell her tree. Soon many people were interested in buying her tree.

Finally, she sold it to an old man. "My dream of my tree reaching to heaven is over," she thought. Her heart was sad.

A few days later, a man came with a big ax and started cutting the tree down. Sofia watched from a distance, with tears flowing down her cheeks.

When the man was done, he put the tree on a wagon and started going towards the city of Jerusalem.

Sofia decided to follow the man to find out what would be done with her tree.

The man stopped by a big building made of wood. There, he started cutting the tree into long, big posts. Sofia quietly watched. Her young heart was full of sadness for her tree.

When the man was done, he continued on his way to the city with the long posts from the tree. Even though Sofia was sad, she was curious to see where the man was going with her tree.

When the man arrived in the city of Jerusalem, Roman soldiers took the long posts made from her tree and put them on the ground. Then, they brought over a different man, who was covered in his own blood and half-naked.

They made him take the posts and put them on his shoulders. Sofia's eyes could not believe what was happening ... her tree was being used to punish someone.

They made the man carry the wood all the way to the top of a hill. There, a soldier nailed the man's hands and feet to the wood and lifted the posts upright, so he was hanging from them. People were laughing and yelling at this poor man, and eventually, he died.

Sofia's heart was broken. "How is this possible?" Sofia thought. Why had she decided to sell her tree?

She felt guilty, and she could not stop crying. Sofia went back to her home, very sad and tired. She fell asleep, hoping that everything was just a bad dream.

The following days, Sofia went outside, sat on the stump where her tree used to be, and cried a little more. She still felt so sad. She did the same for several days, missing her tree and wishing she had never sold it.

A few days passed. Again, Sofia went out and sat on the tree stump, still feeling very sad and guilty for selling the tree. While she was lost in her thoughts, someone touched her shoulder. When she turned around to see who it was, her eyes could not believe who was standing beside her.

It was the same man the Roman soldier had nailed to the wood and had died on the hill! Sofia was speechless, but the man told her,

"Sofia, do not worry!" He gave her a hug.

The man sat by her and started explaining to her exactly what she saw a few days before.

Would you like to know what the man told her?

The man told Sofia that his name was Jesus and that her special tree was part of God's important plan from the beginning of time. Jesus explained that he came to die on the cross and come back to life so that anyone who believes in him can have a very special kind of life—eternal life. That is the kind of life that lasts forever and ever with God in heaven. Jesus said his death would bring that special life to many people.

Then Jesus thanked Sofia for giving her tree and explained that with it, he was able to accomplish God's very important plan of offering eternal life to everyone.

"Sofia don't be sad you saw me dying. Now you see me here, I conquered death and I want to offer eternal life to you too. Will you believe in me? Will you let me into your heart?"

Sofia said, "Yes!"

Then the man said, "Sofia, I will be with you always," and started walking away.

He turned to Sofia one last time and said, "Sofia, remember your dream of your tree reaching to heaven? That dream has come true today."

Sofia's heart was happy again! She was no longer sad. Her tree was part of this amazing plan, and yes, her tree was reaching up to heaven! Sofia ran inside her home and told her family what happened, and they all believed and received Jesus in their hearts!!!

Do you want to ask Jesus into your heart?

Today ___/____/___

I, ...received Jesus into my heart and my

....

presented the salvation story to me.

Draw a picture or write something to remember this time!!! And memorize this bible verse: For God so loved the world, that He gave His only begotten Son, that whoever believes in Him shall not perish, but have eternal life. John 3:16 NASB